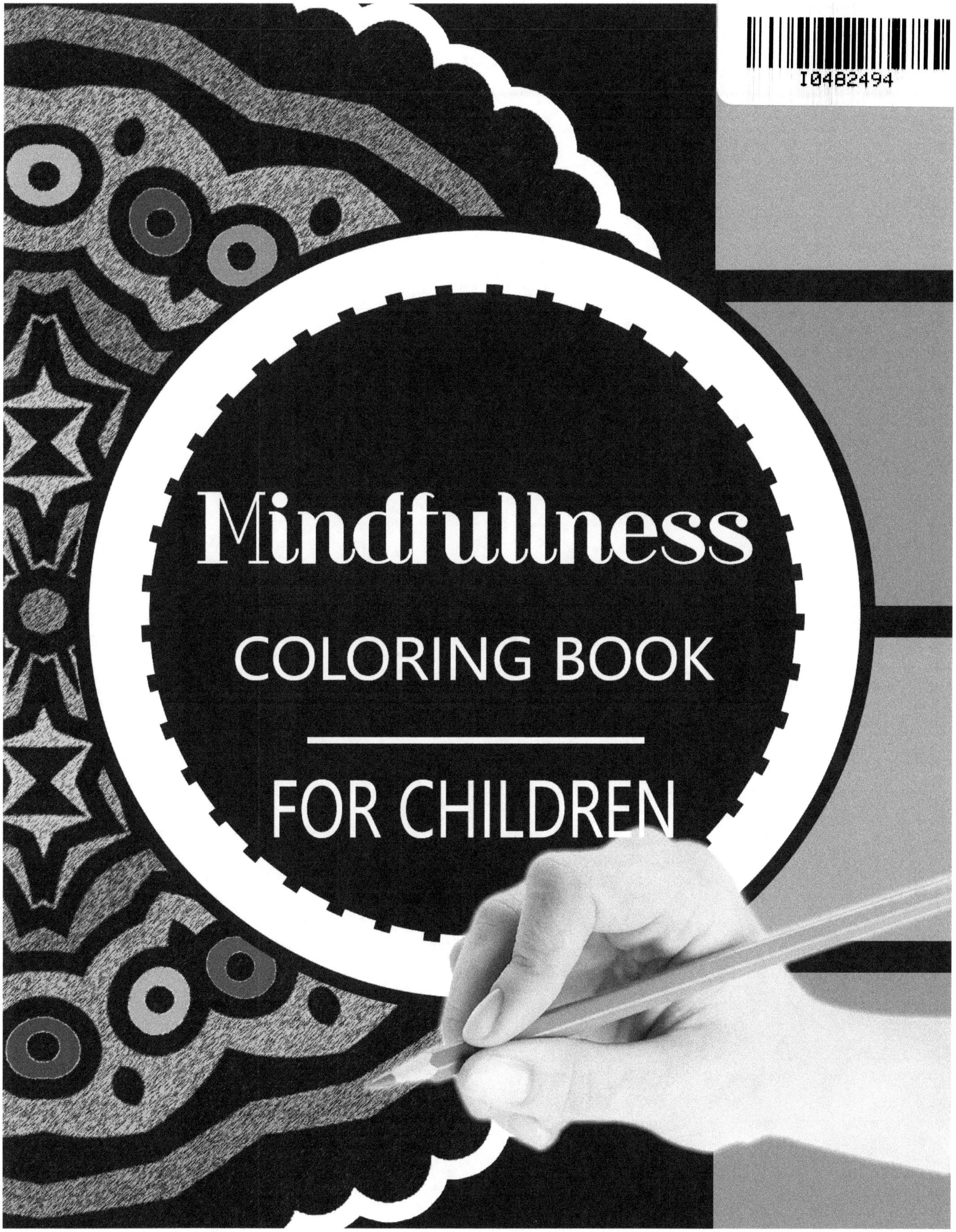
Mindfullness
COLORING BOOK
FOR CHILDREN

COLOR TEST PAGE

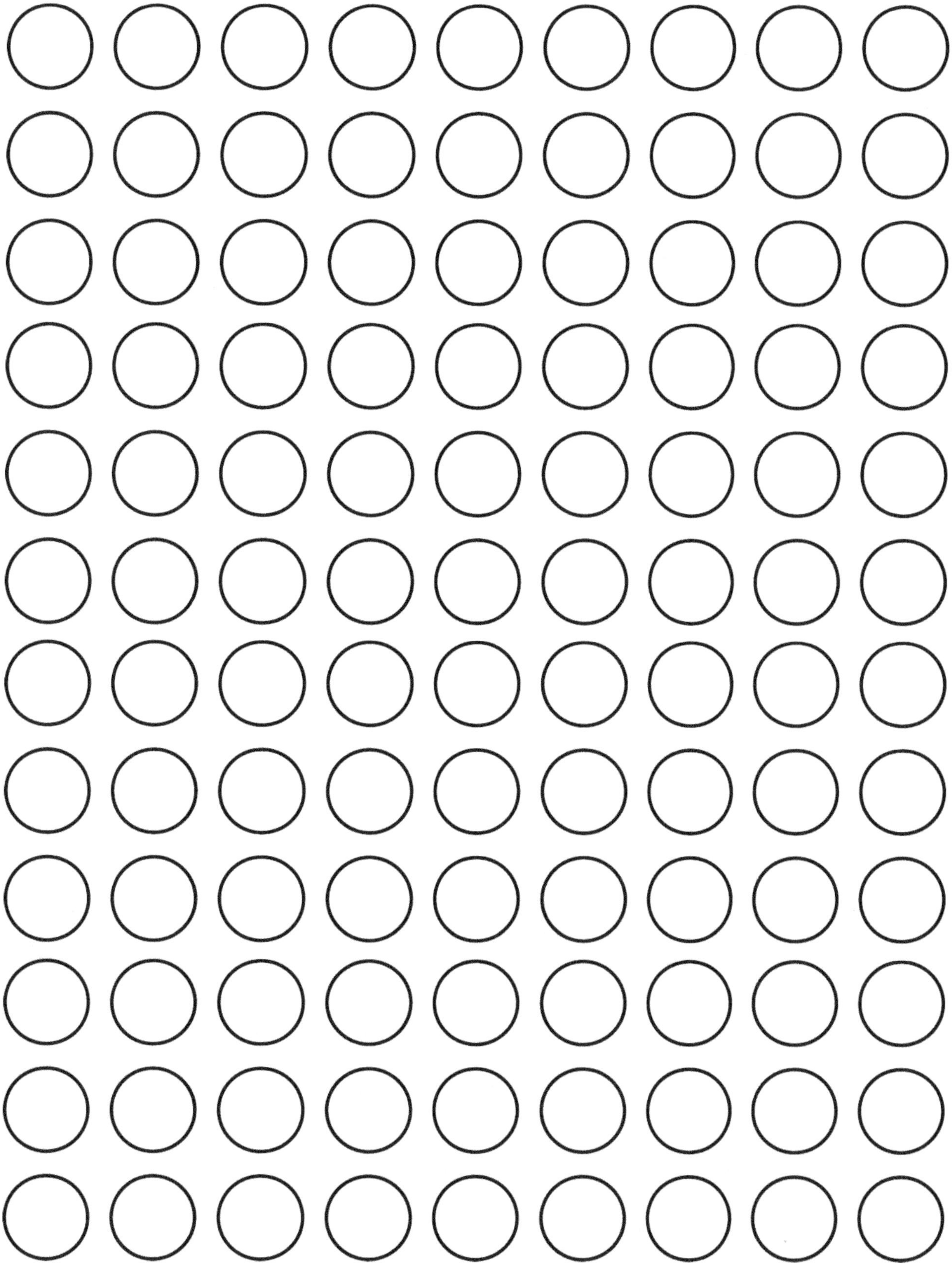

COLOR TEST PAGE

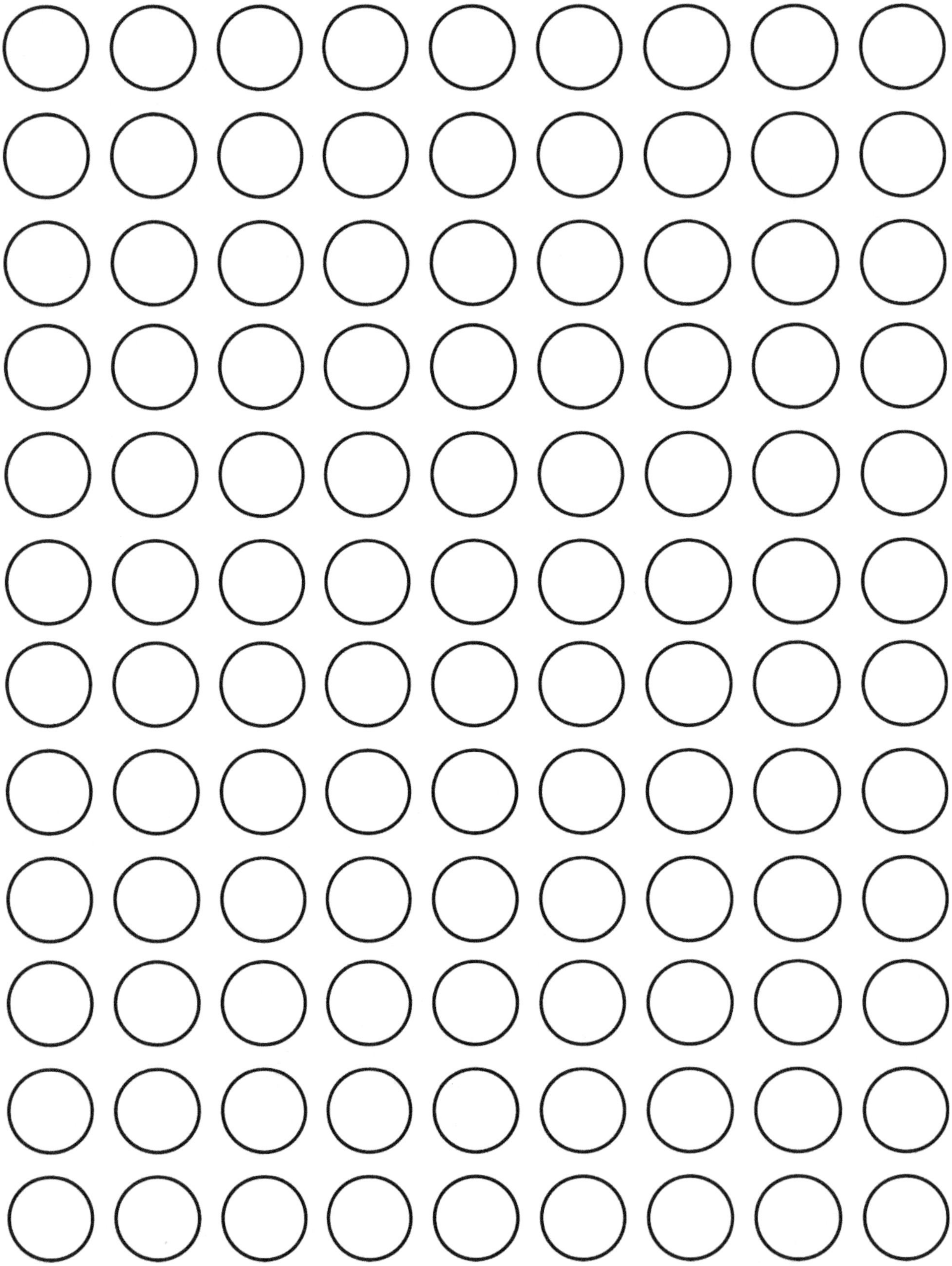

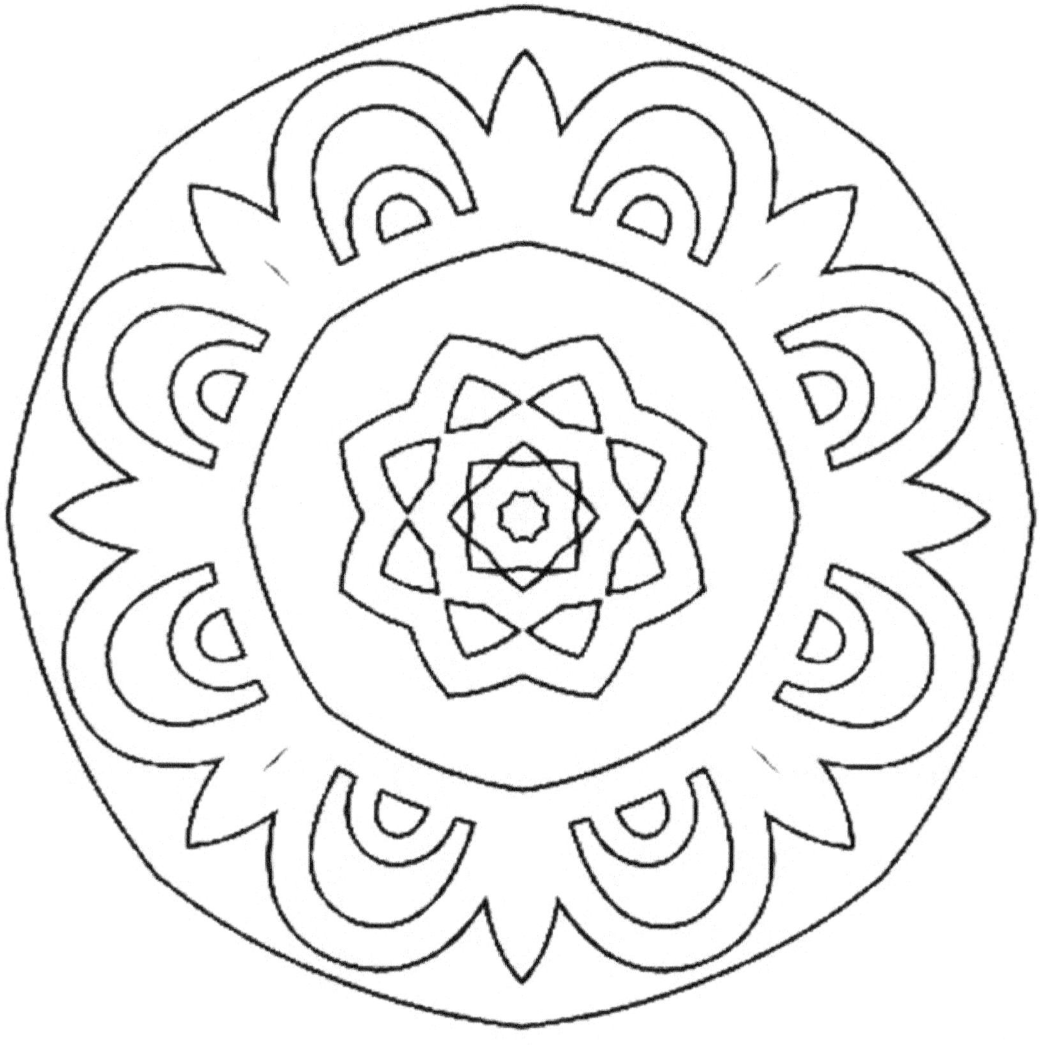

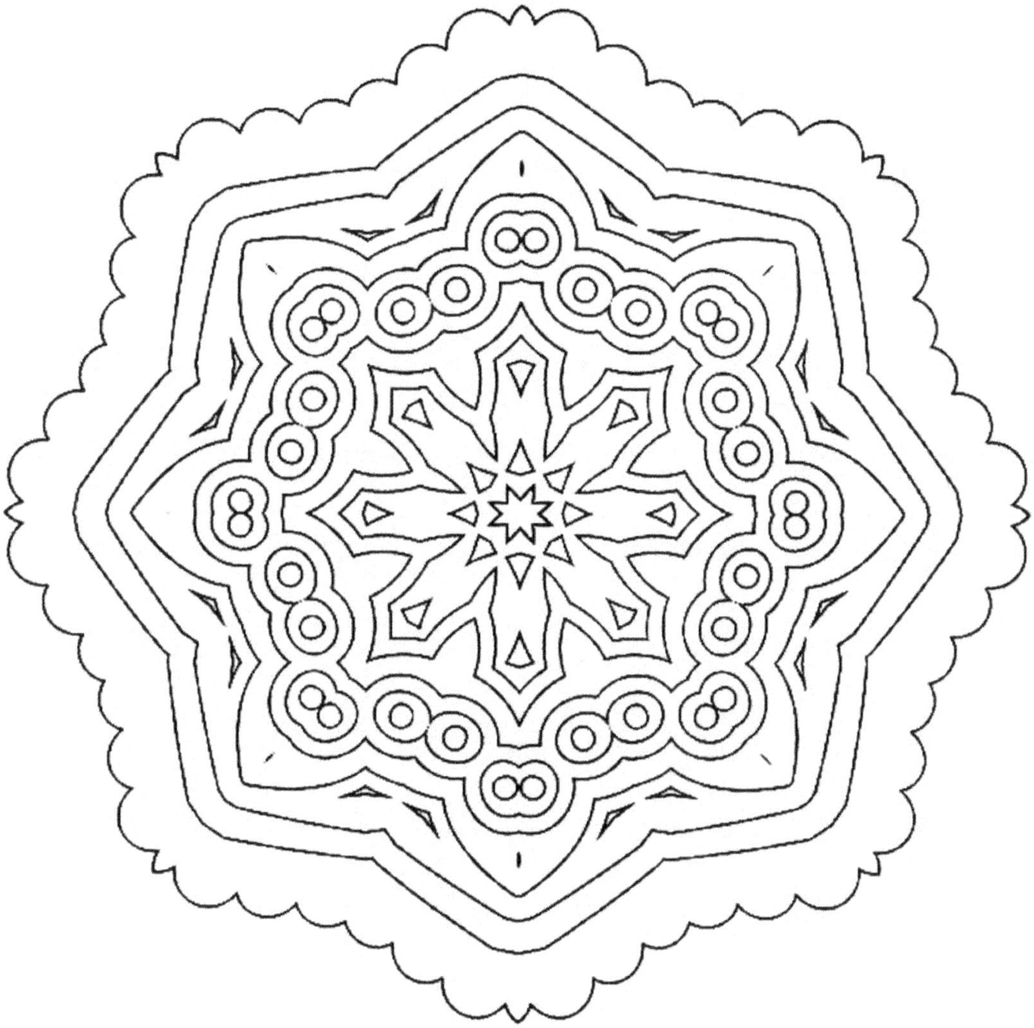

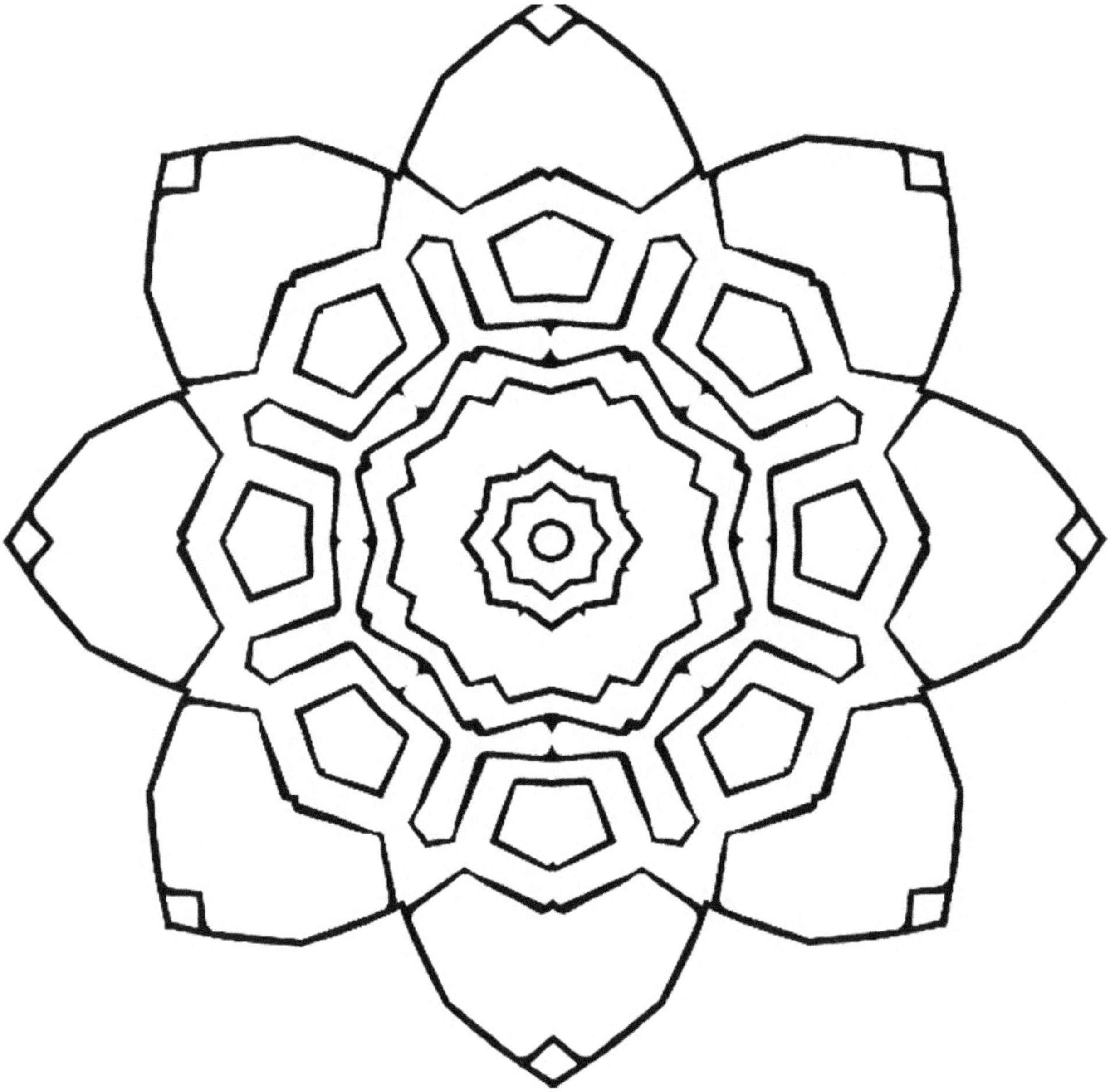

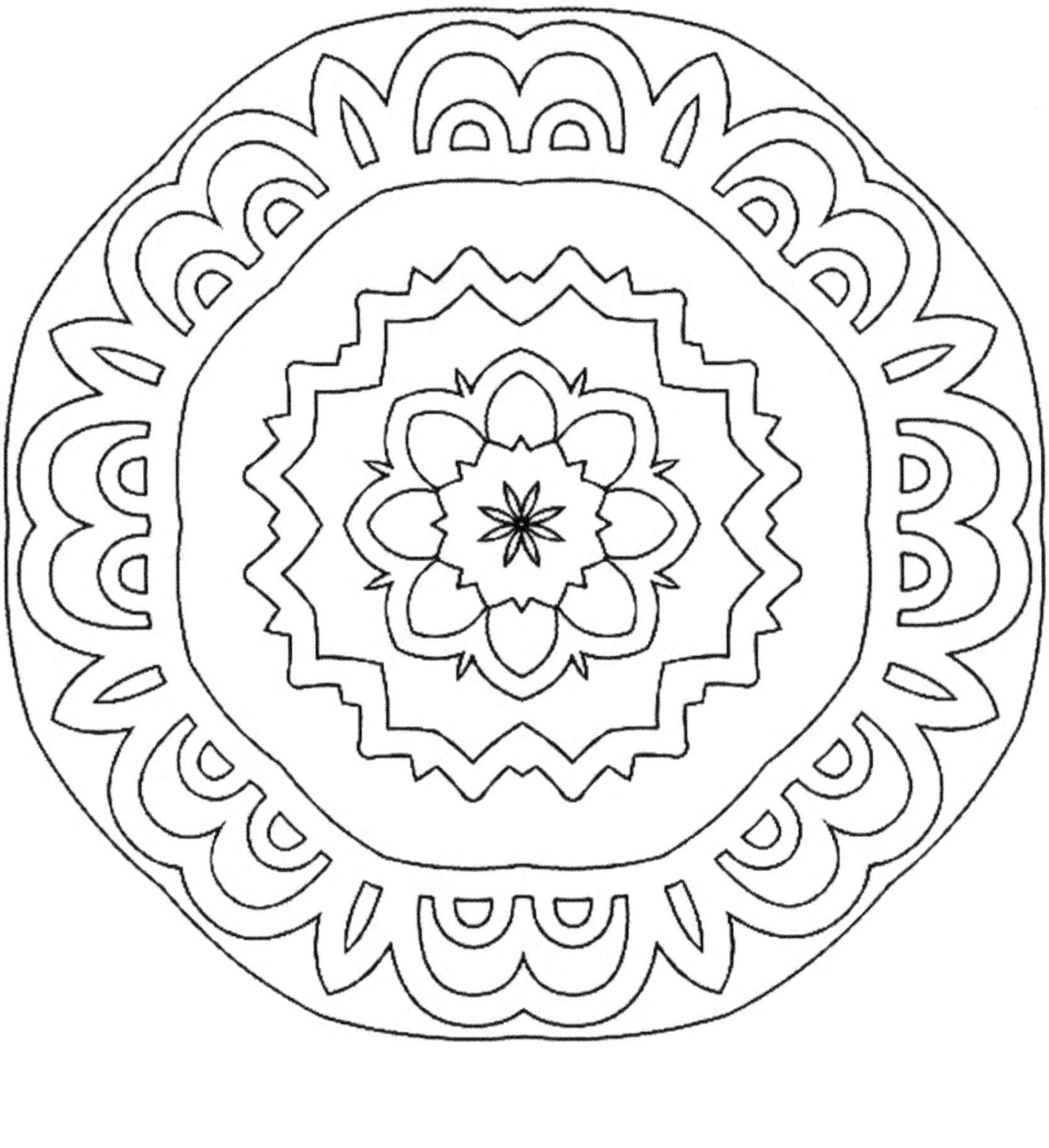

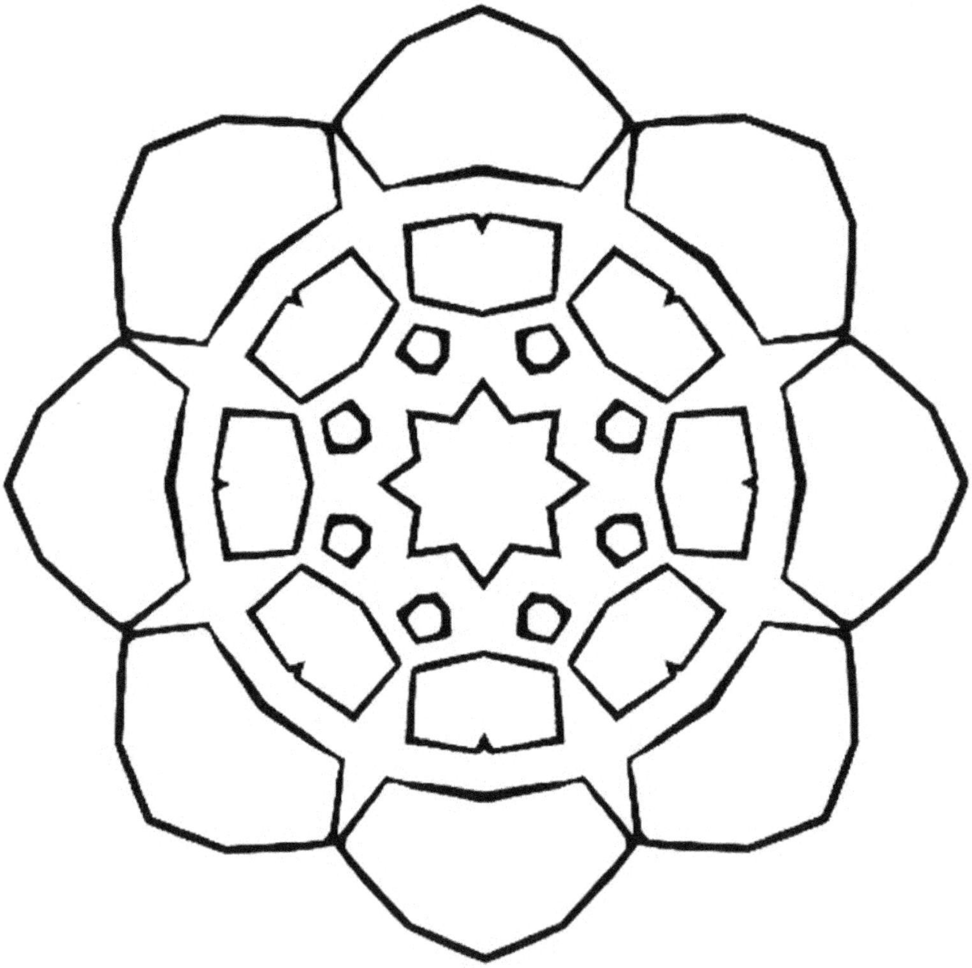

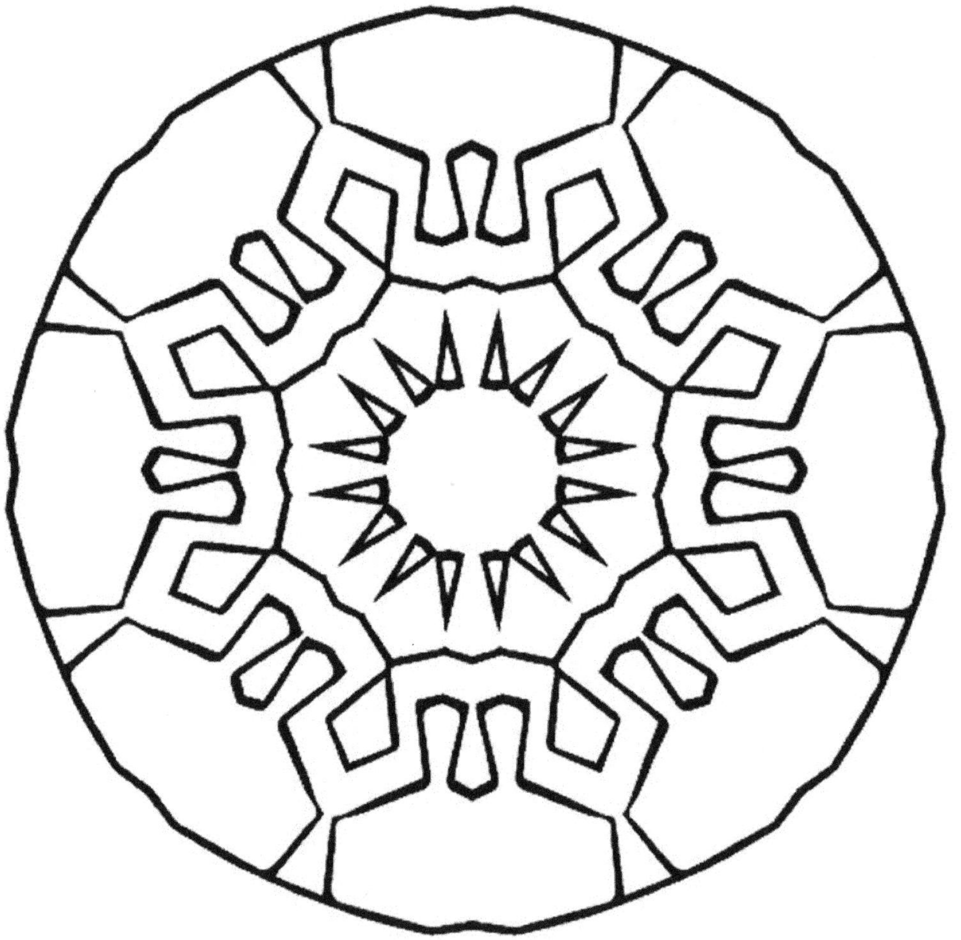

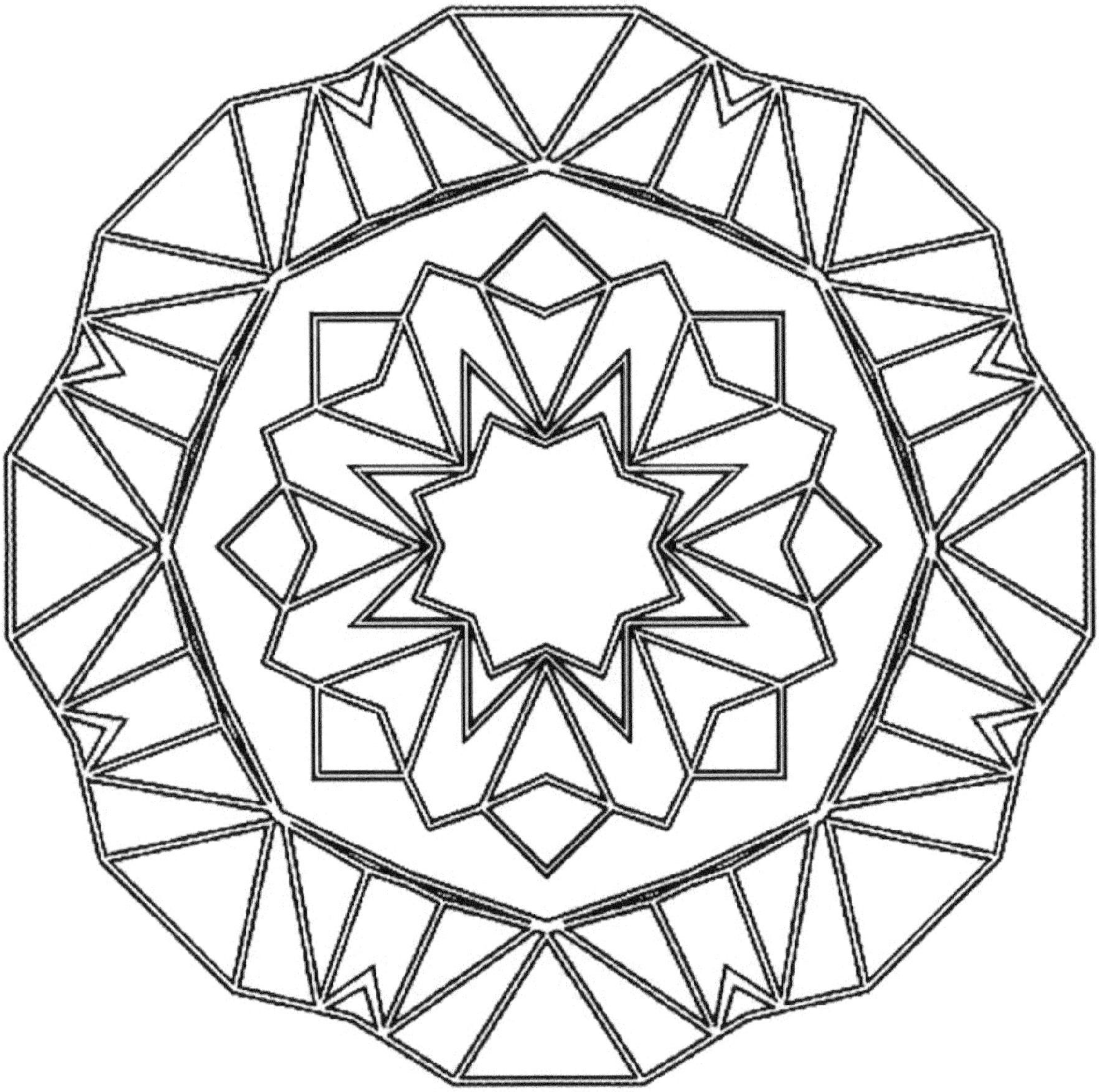

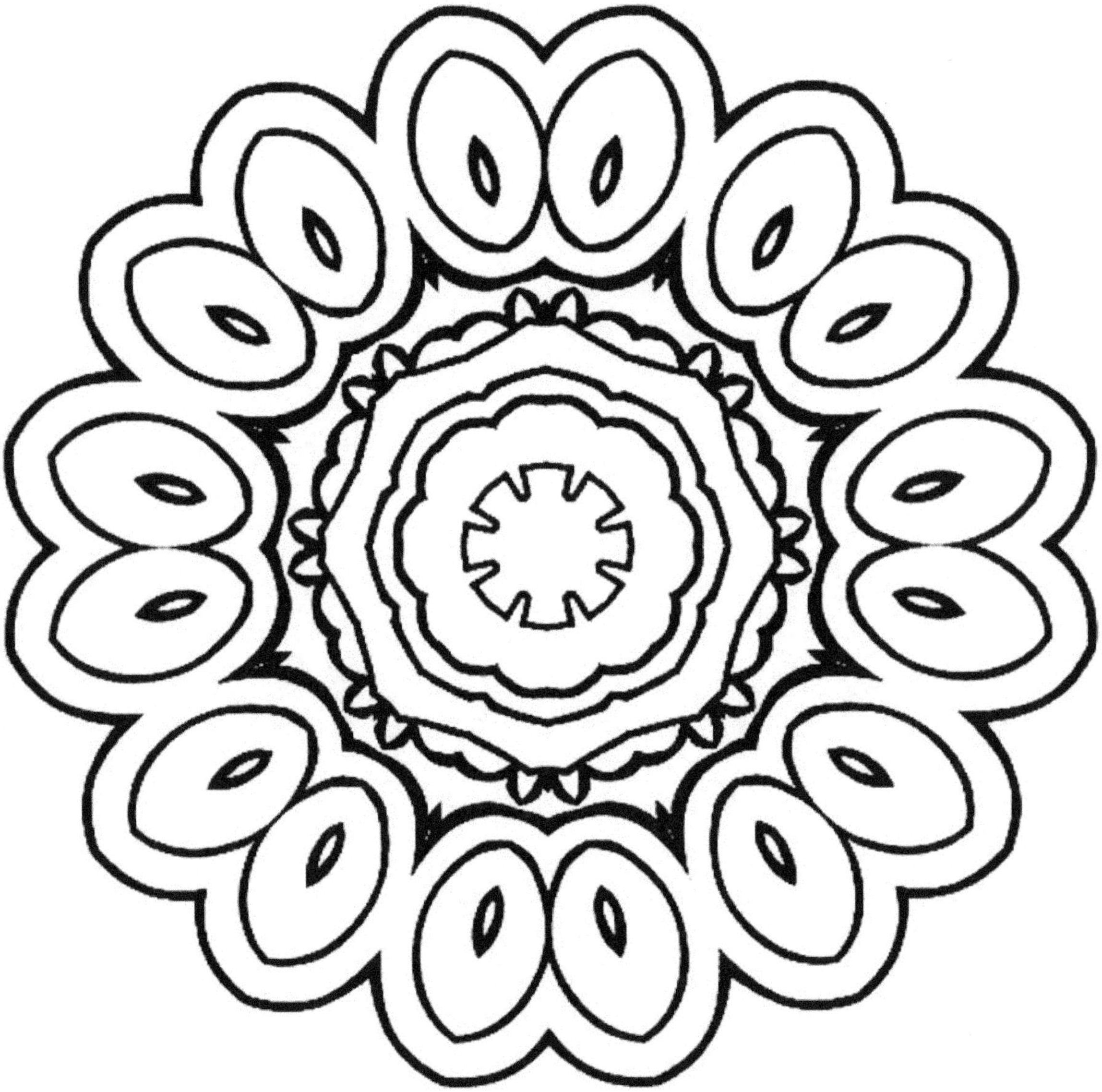

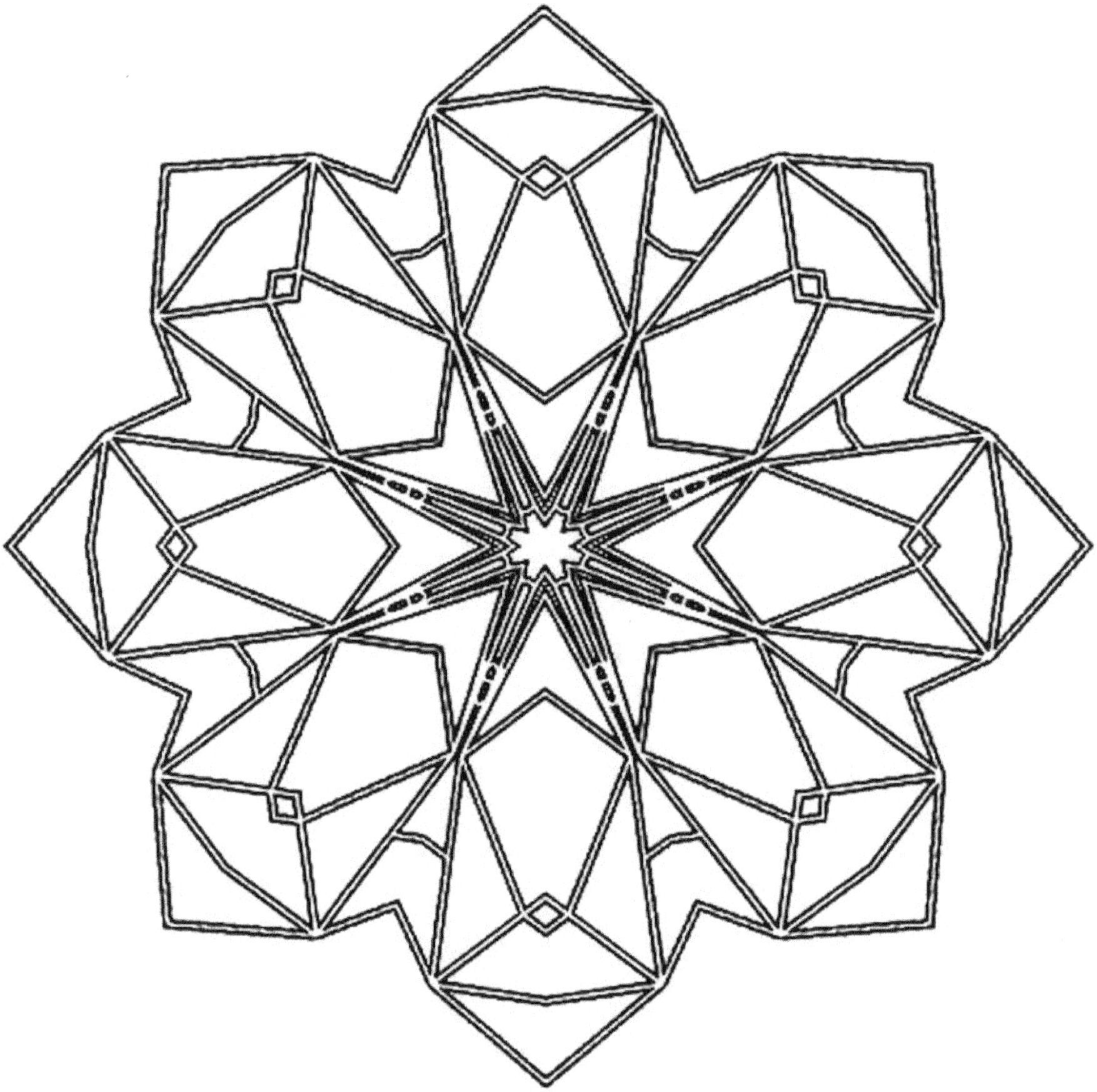

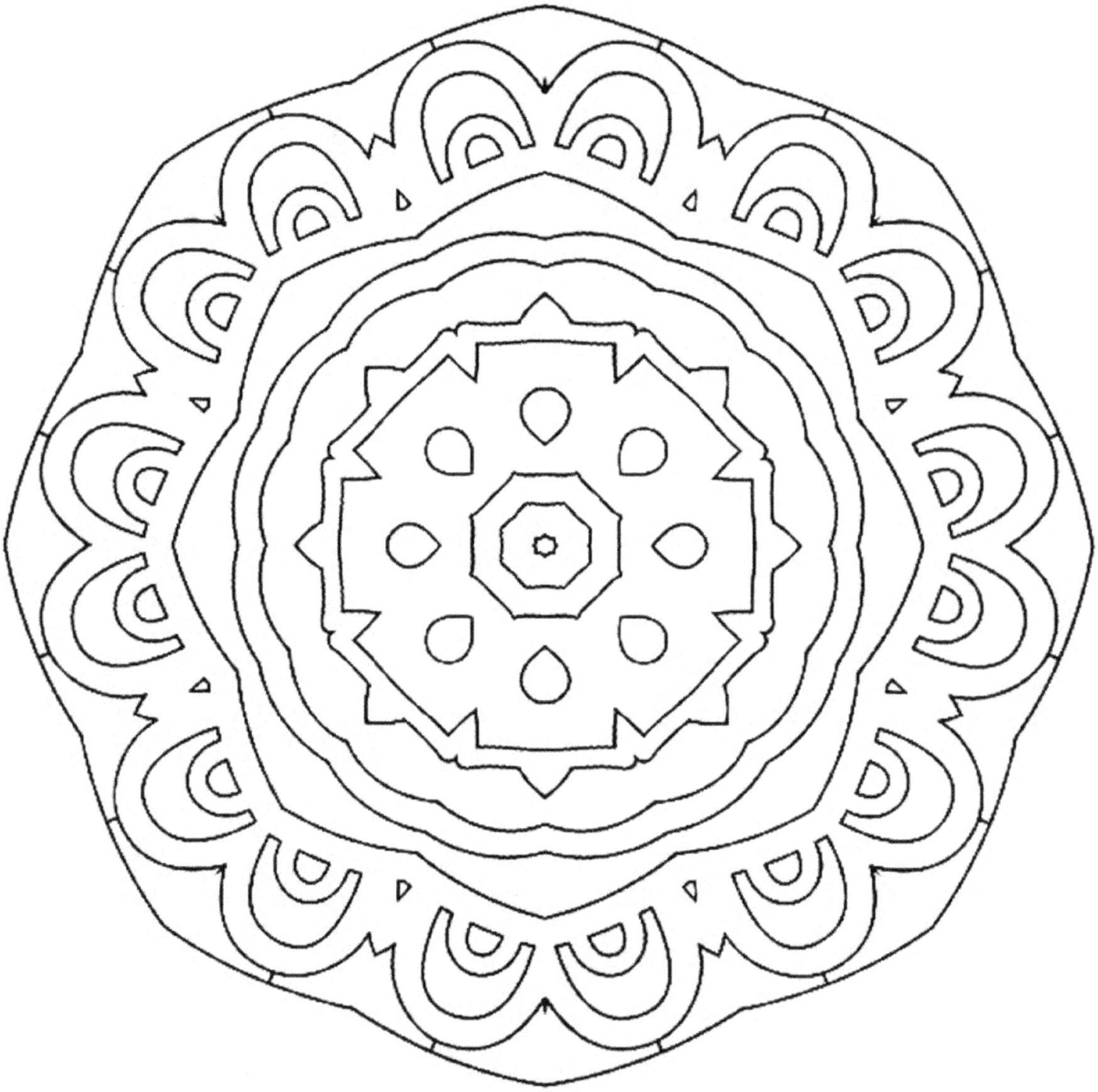

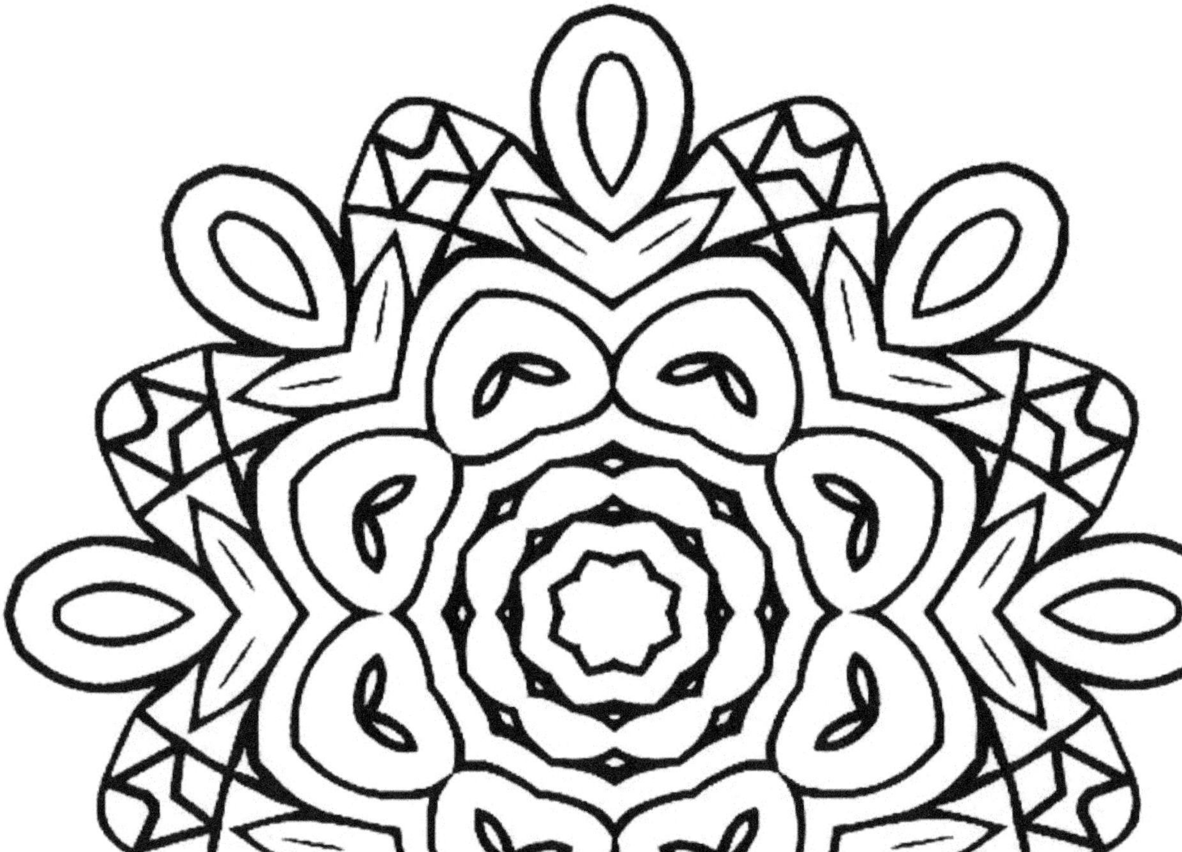

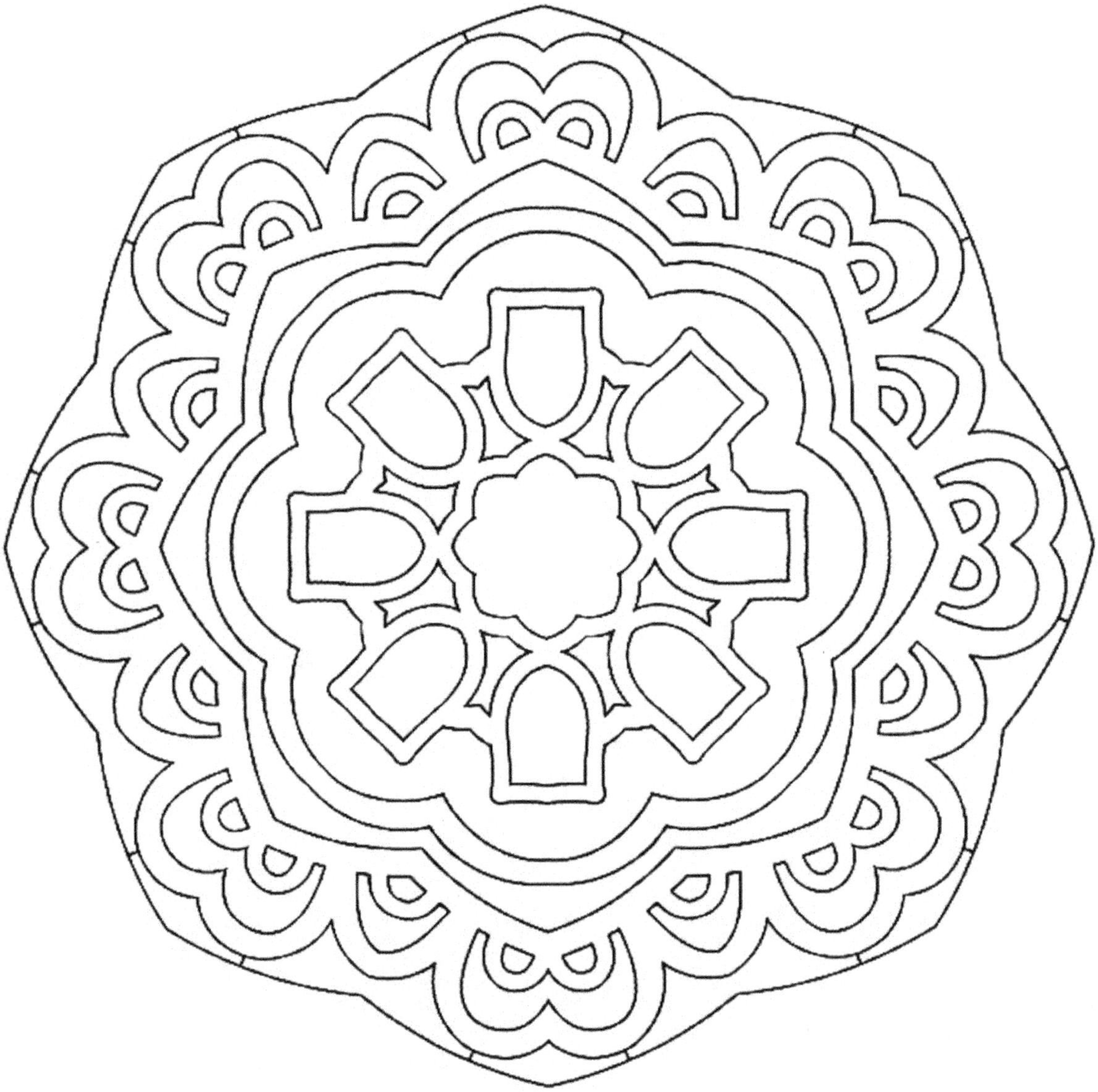

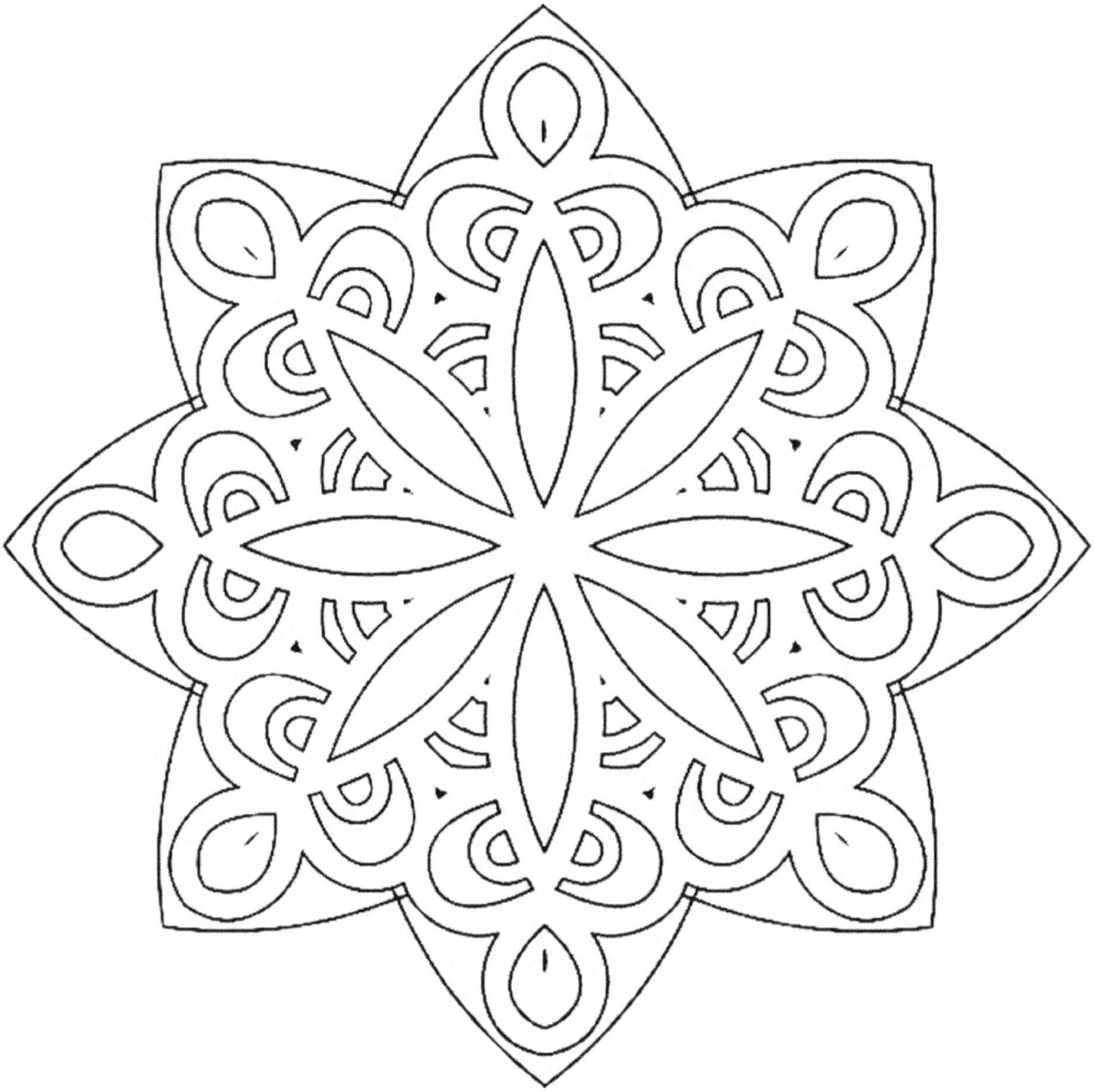

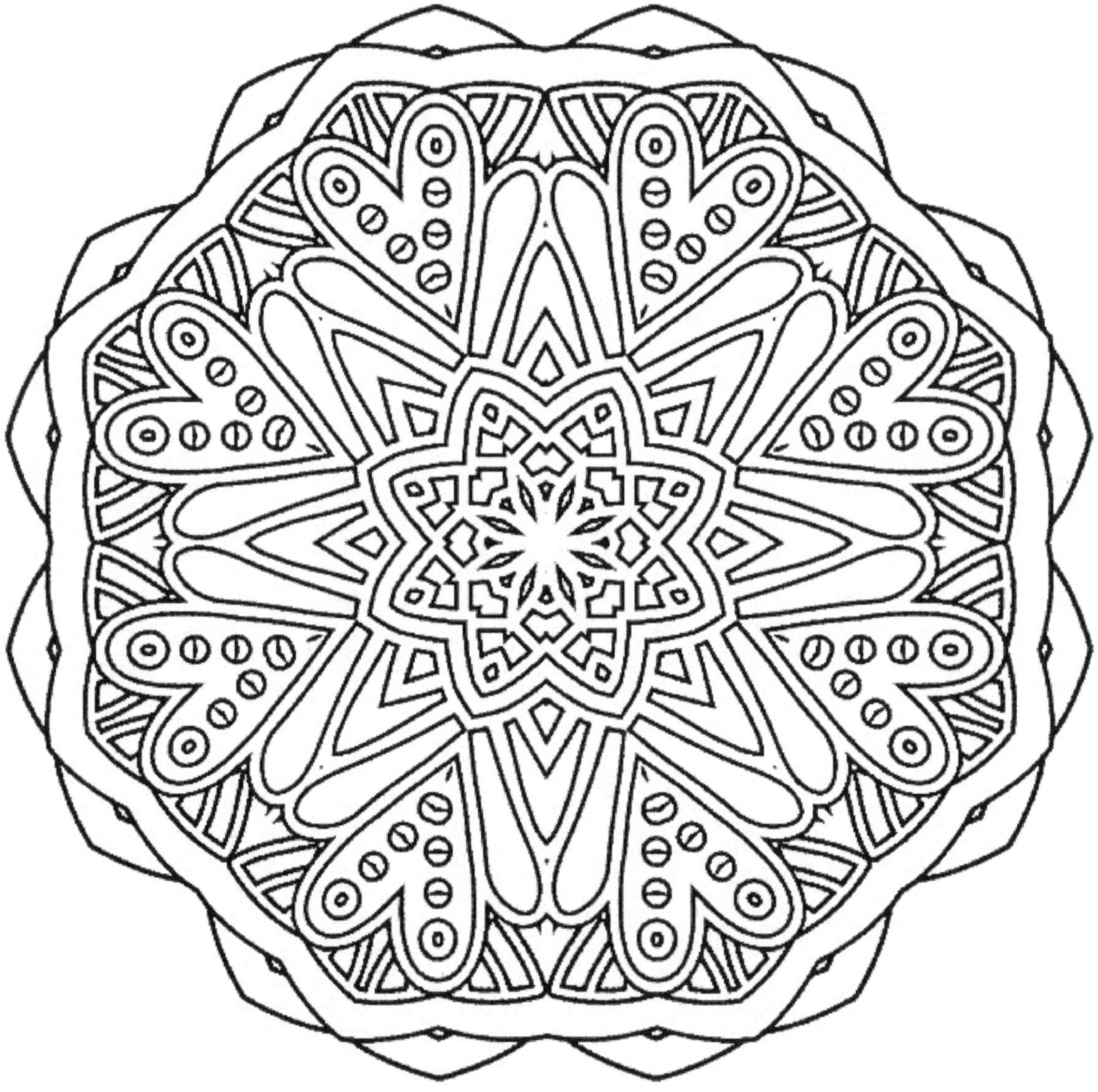

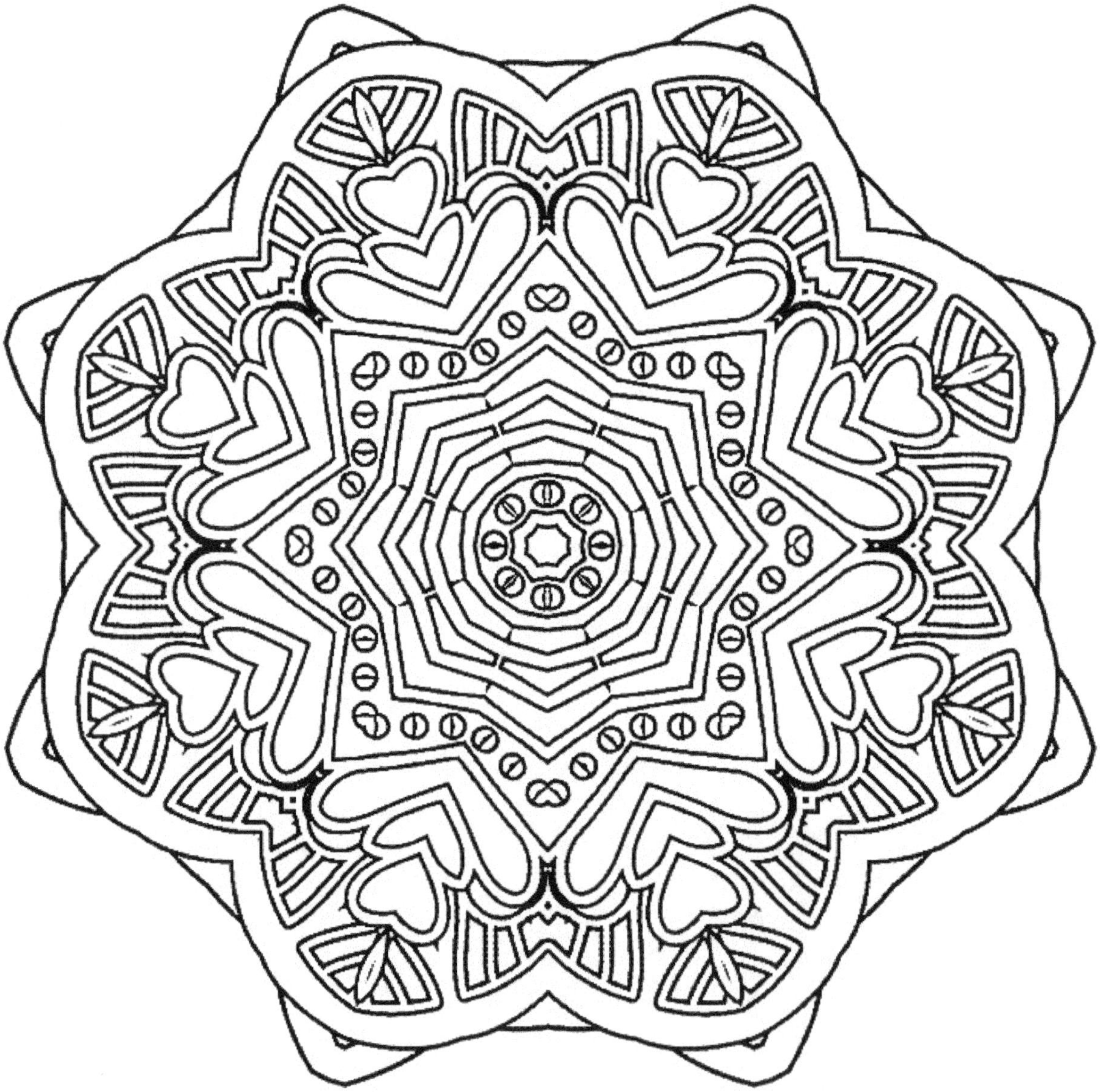

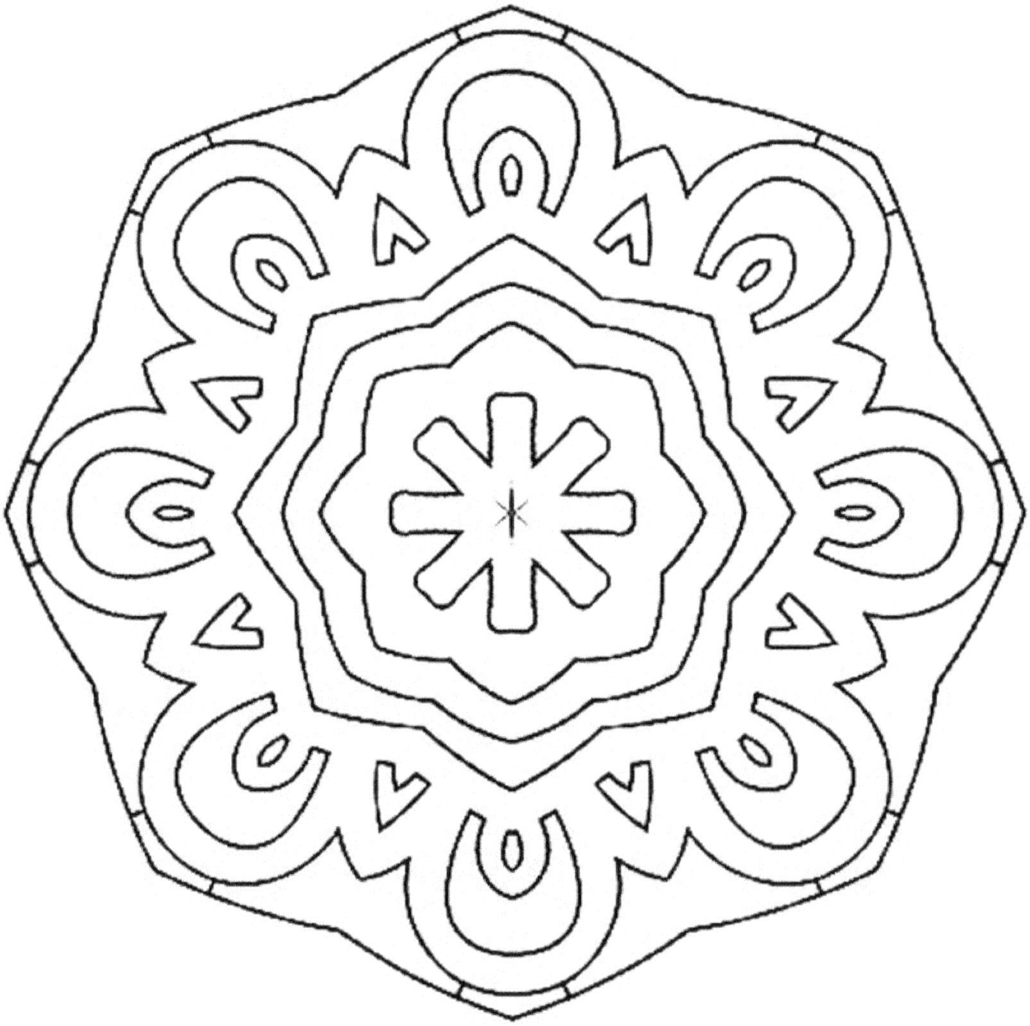

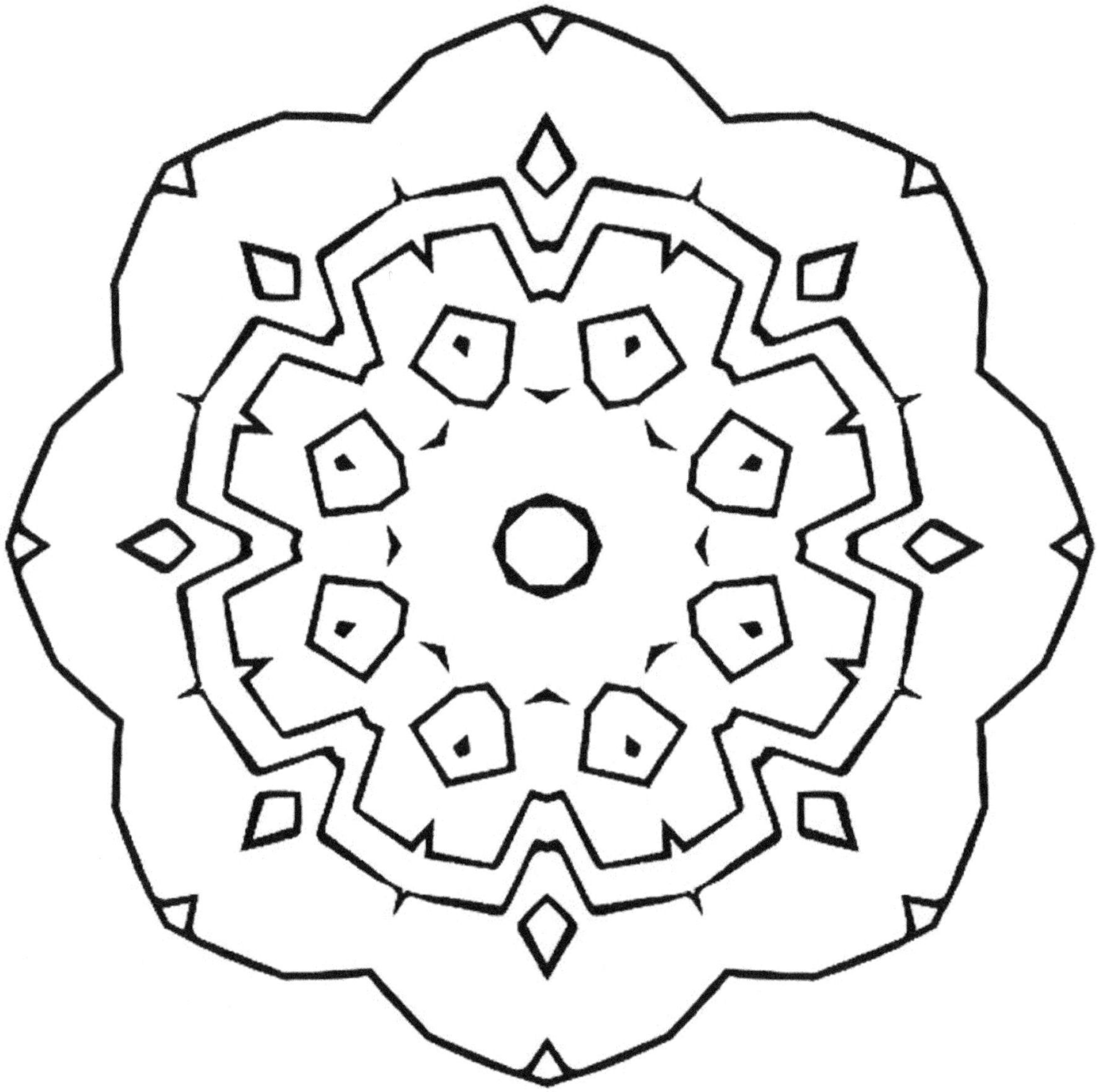

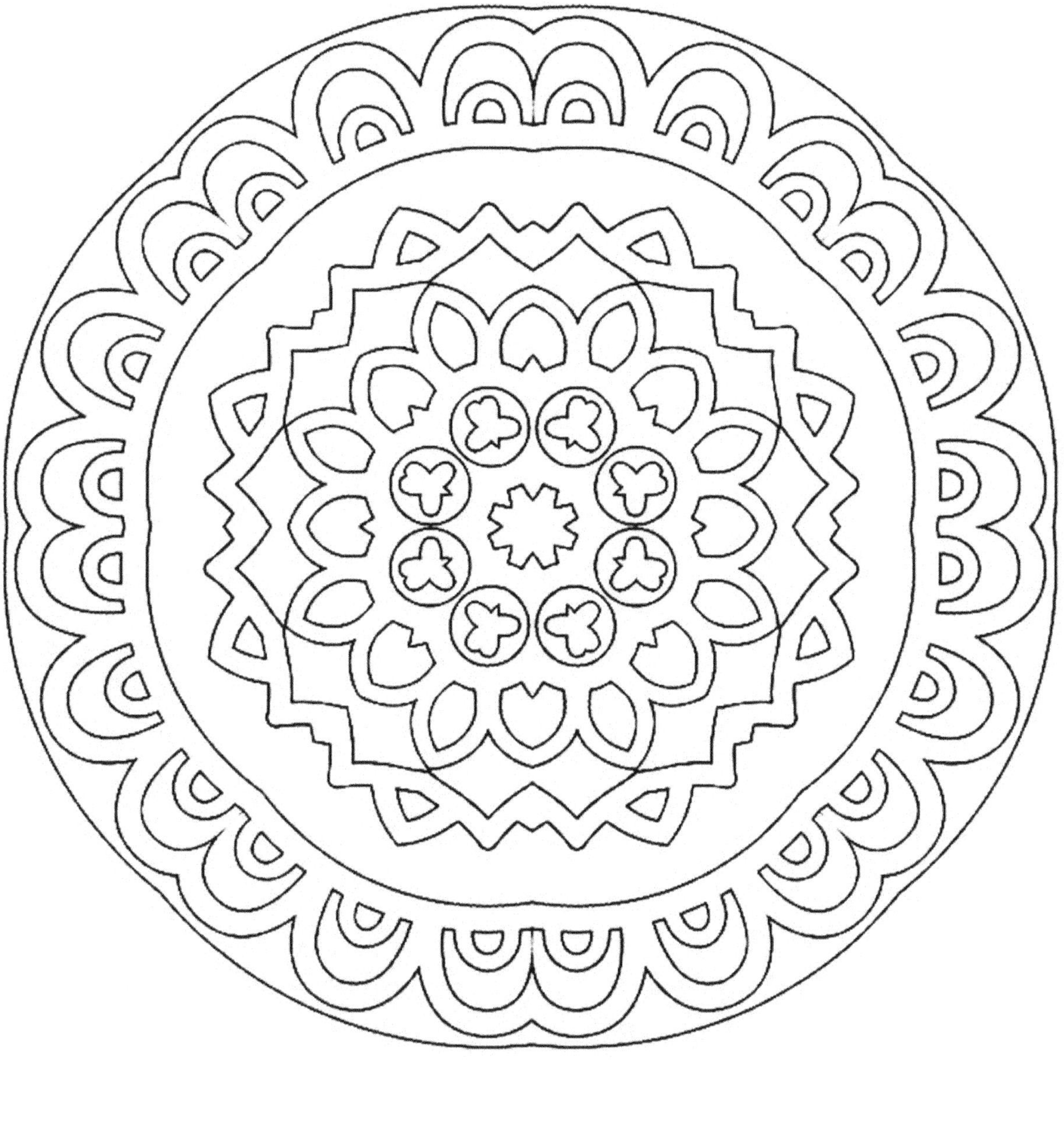

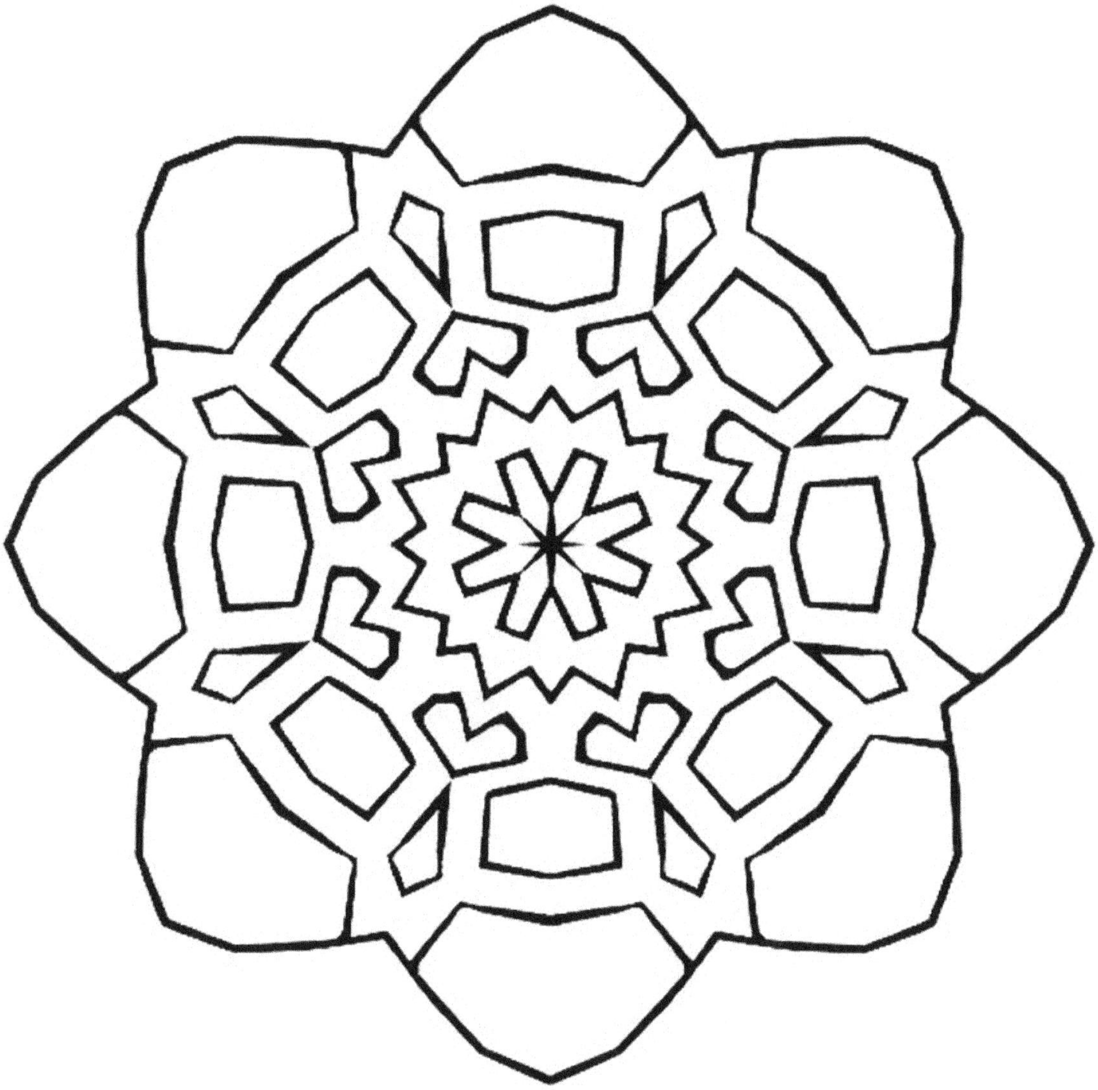

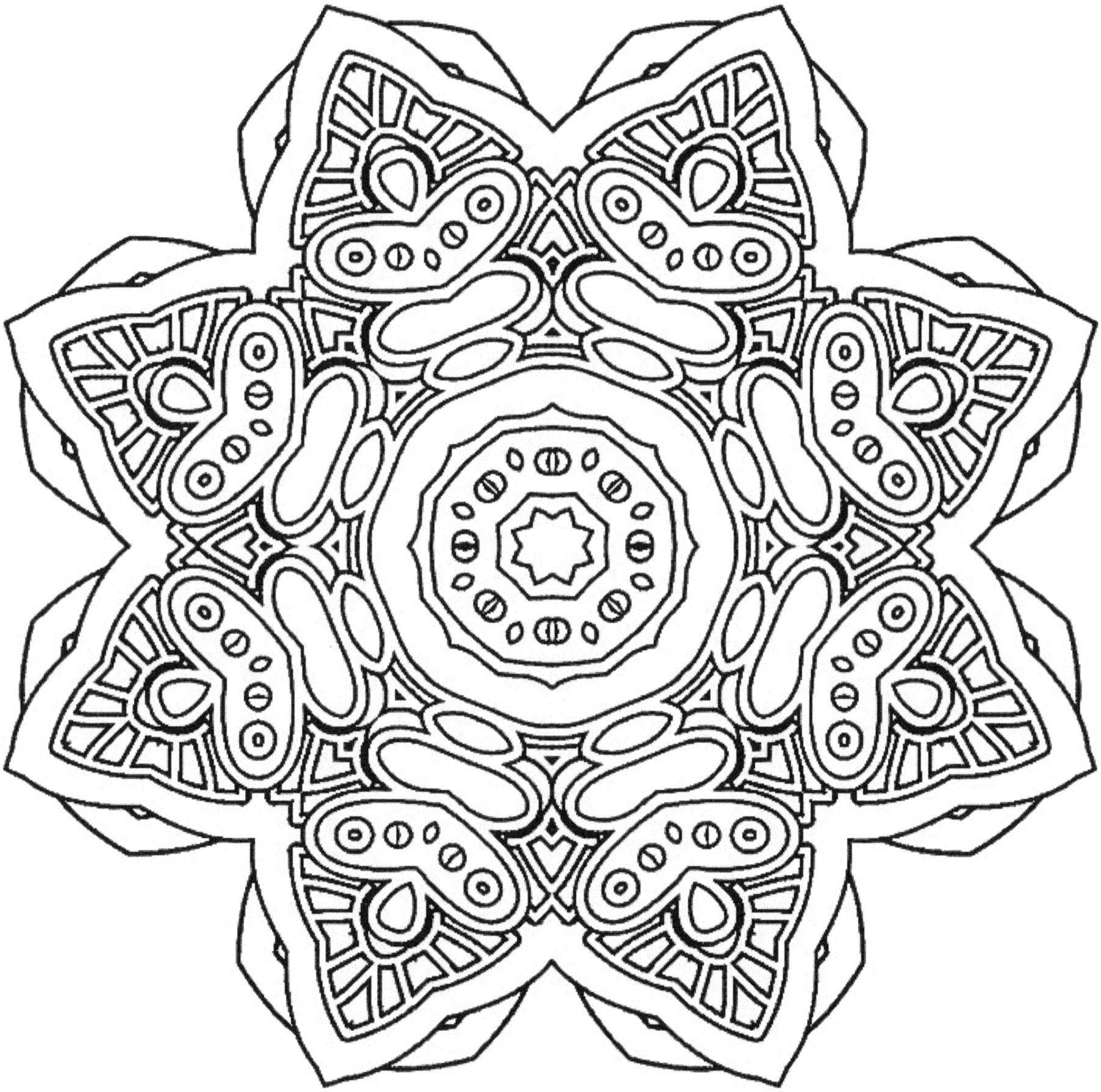

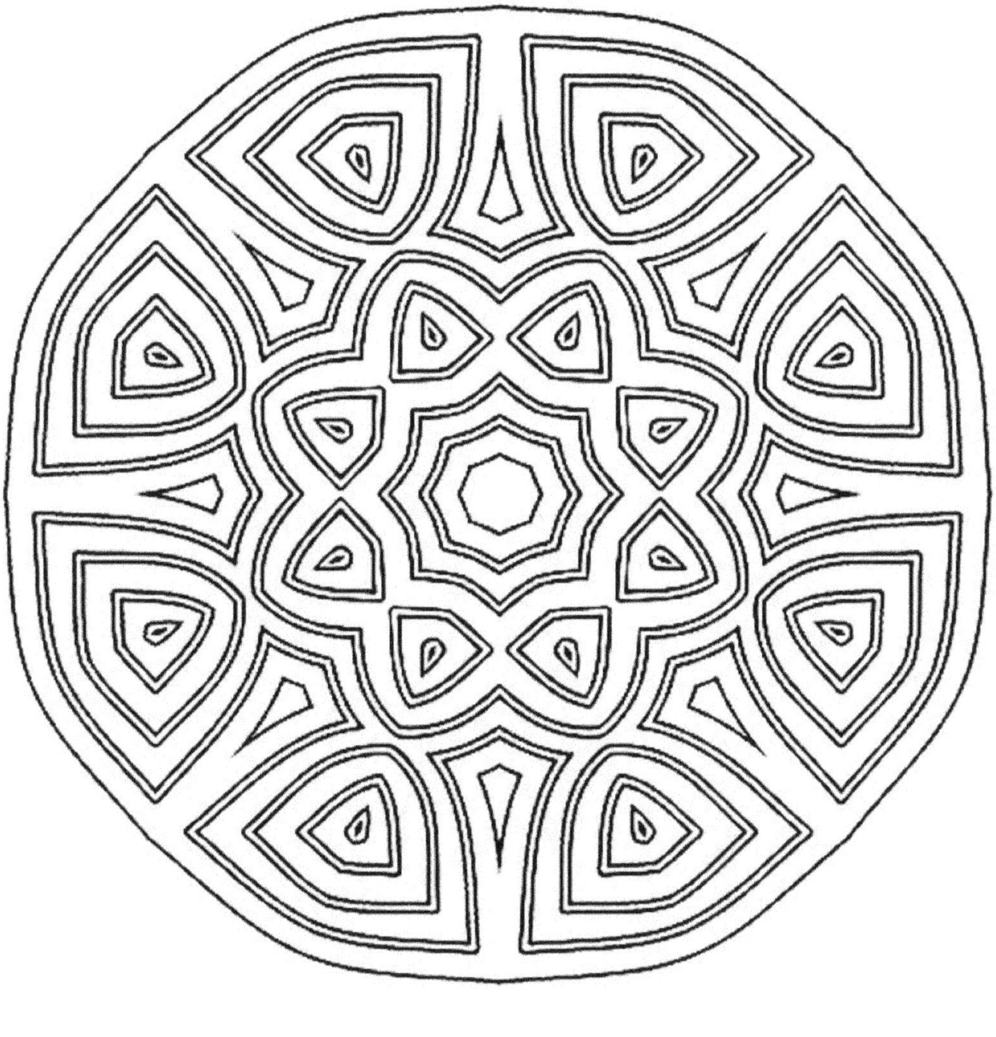

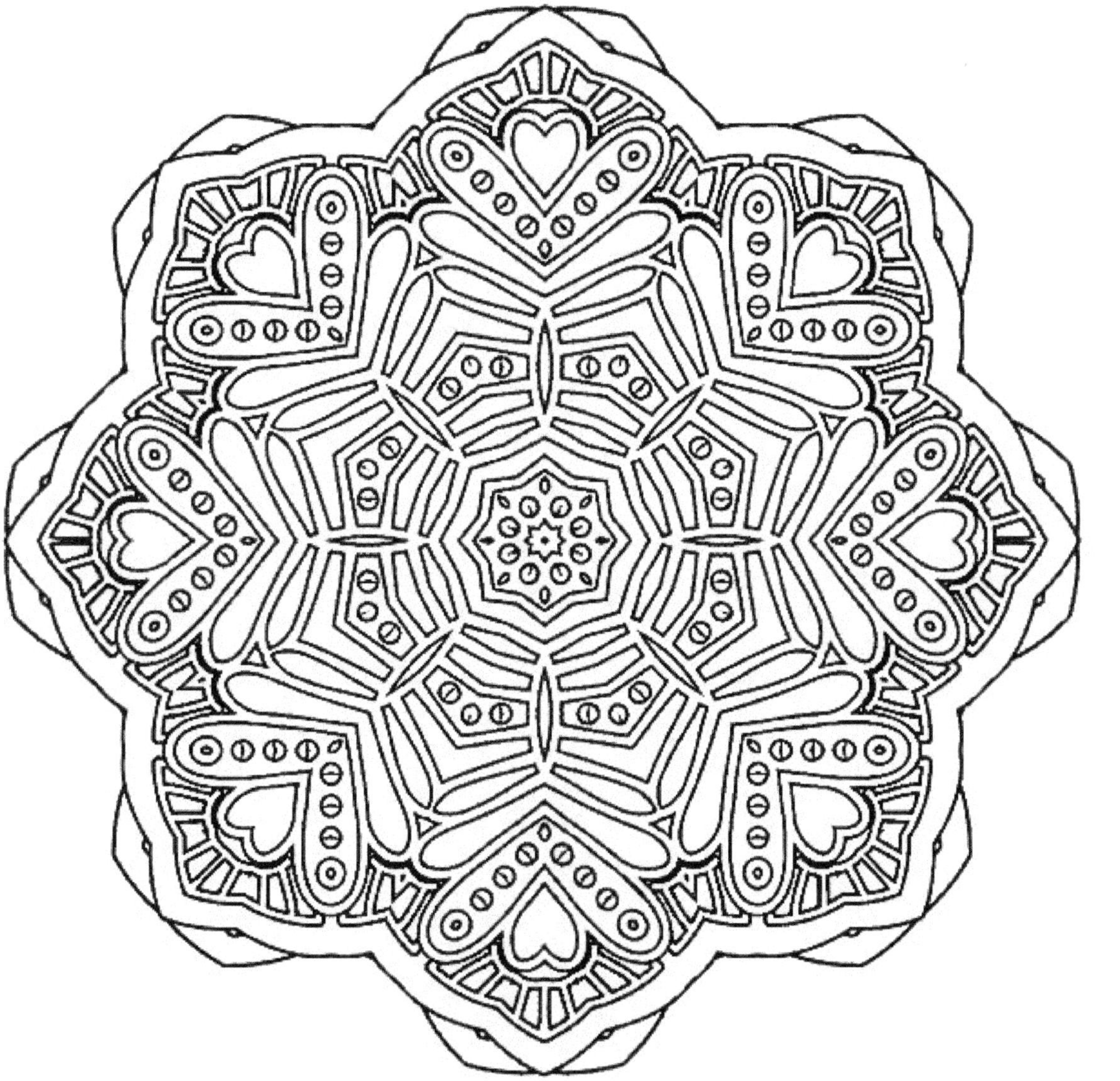

www.ingramcontent.com/pod-product-compliance
Lightning Source LLC
Chambersburg PA
CBHW080607190526
45169CB00007B/2919
9781534798601